JOURNEY TO FREEDOM
Study Guide Series

JOURNEY

TO A NEW BEGINNING AFTER A LOSS

Freedom from the Pain of
Grief and Disappointment

YMCA OF MIDDLE TENNESSEE
SCOTT REALL

THOMAS NELSON
Since 1798

NASHVILLE   DALLAS   MEXICO CITY   RIO DE JANEIRO   BEIJING

Published in Nashville, Tennessee, by Thomas Nelson. Thomas Nelson is a registered trademark of Thomas Nelson, Inc.

Thomas Nelson, Inc., titles may be purchased in bulk for educational, business, fund-raising, or sales promotional use. For information, please e-mail SpecialMarkets@ThomasNelson.com.

Scripture quotations marked NCV are from New Century Version®. © 2005 by Thomas Nelson, Inc. Used by permission. All rights reserved.

Scripture quotations marked NLT are from *Holy Bible*, New Living Translation. © 1996. Used by permission of Tyndale House Publishers, Inc., Wheaton, Illinois 60189. All rights reserved.

Scripture quotations marked NIV are from THE HOLY BIBLE: NEW INTERNATIONAL VERSION®. © 1973, 1978, 1984 by International Bible Society. Used by permission of Zondervan Publishing House. All rights reserved.

To find a YMCA near you, please visit the following Web sites:

United States of America: www.ymca.com
Canada: www.ymca.ca
England: www.ymca.org.uk
Australia: www.ymca.org.au

Visit www.restoreymca.org for more information on Restore, a life-changing ministry of the YMCA.

ISBN 978-1-4185-0771-8

Printed in the United States of America.
08 09 10 11 RRD 5 4 3 2 1

CONTENTS

In the movie *On the Waterfront*, Marlon Brando's character shows promise as a champion boxer, but his brother dashes his boxing dreams. In one poignant scene, Brando has taken a dive for his brother, missing his chance to be victorious in a match that would have made him famous. He says to his brother, "You was my brother, Charlie, you shoulda looked out for me. You shoulda taken care of me just a little bit so I wouldn't have to take the dive. You don't understand, I coulda had class. I coulda been a contender. I coulda been somebody. Instead of a bum. Which is what I am, let's face it. It was you, Charlie."[1]

This scene resonates with me because I've had this conversation with myself. "Scott, you should have looked out for yourself. You should have paid attention. You could have been a champion. You could have been a contender. You could have been somebody. You should have reached for your dreams."

I wonder how many people out there have these same feelings? They've missed their dreams, or life has turned out tragically different from what they had hoped it would be. Or perhaps they've lost a loved one, and certain dreams died with that person. As long as we live, life is about loss. In *Unmasking Male Depression*, Archibald D. Hart writes,

> All of life is loss. It starts the day we are born, when we lose the safety and comfort of the womb. Never again will we be as safe as there, protected by our mother's immune system and the placenta.

As we grow older, the potential for loss increases daily. When we graduate from kindergarten, we leave behind a safe place and special friends. When we transition from adolescence to adulthood, we again lose a degree of freedom and carefreeness. When we start to earn some money, we make investments and may lose all that hard-earned money. Very much later, we begin to lose our faculties, eyesight, teeth, and hair. Finally, we lose life itself. Life is all about loss—necessary losses.[2]

My parents taught me to strive for things. They educated my siblings and I in the importance of following our dreams. But they didn't teach us that dreams often end, and we need to learn how to grieve them. That's the theme of Longfellow's poem, "My Lost Youth":

> *There are things of which I may not speak*
> *There are dreams that cannot die*
> *There are thoughts that make the strong heart weak*
> *And bring a pallor into the cheek*
> *And a mist before the eye*
> *And the words of that fatal song come over me like a chill*
> *A boy's will is the wind's will*
> *And the thoughts of youth are long, long thoughts*[3]

Farah Moore and Sheryl Cooke, authors of the book, *From Hurt to Hope*, suggest we are only taught how to strive for success, but we are never taught how to handle loss. Striving to get things and believing we can hold onto them is an illusion. Everything we have in this life will one day be lost. Beloved pets will die. Our parents will most likely pass away before we do. We will have to retire from a job that we might love.

Moore and Cooke write, "Unresolved emotions, from disappointments, losses, and hurts, weigh me down, distract me, and hinder my progress."[4] These unresolved emotions sabotage our ability to live fully in the present, as God intended. But if we learn to grieve effectively and appropriately, we can arrive at new beginnings and continue our journeys with free hearts. In this book we will walk through the five stages of the grieving process—denial, anger, bargaining, depression/sadness, and then acceptance. Each stage is necessary in the healing of our grief.

There is a way through loss. You don't have to carry grief like a soldier. You might feel as though your problems are too small and insignificant to discuss, but getting them out in the open among a group of safe people can be healing. Burdens always become lighter when others help us carry them. My hope for you as you study this guide is that this will be the beginning of help, hope, and healing for your life. Even though your grief may never vanish completely, you can learn to deal with it in healthy ways.

Most of the people we've worked with over the last ten years at Restore Ministries came to us with broken hearts. Their dreams had died or had been ripped away. But the people who allow their hearts to be broken openly before God are able to move forward. Those who refuse to accept loss will never move forward. They shield broken hearts they need to expose. This sort of denial keeps its victims trapped. So be honest in examining your loss as you move through this study. How you approach this can mean the difference between a new beginning or the same defeated past. It's time to live!

CHAPTER ONE

LOSS AND DENIAL

Living with loss begins in childhood—it begins simply with the loss of a favorite toy or the attention of our parents. Then we lose at sports, or perhaps we lose a pet. We eventually lose our innocence. But when we lose a parent or a grandparent or some significant person in our lives, the loss becomes major. The *Grief Recovery Handbook* says that loss is cumulative.[1] Think of a glass slightly filled with emotional pain. Each time a new loss presents itself—and is not worked through—the glass gets more full. Suffer enough losses and the cup runs over. This presents the image of major grief. As we discuss losses, both minor and major, in this study, we will come to understand a hope beyond the losses we suffer in this world. This hope is available to us all. I've discovered it in my own life, and I'll share some of my experiences.

LOSS OF DREAMS

Childhood is a magical time. Virtually your entire life is ahead of you. Anything and everything seems possible. When I was in the backyard throwing a football, I was dreaming of becoming a football player. When I was at my first dance in eighth grade, I was dreaming of my first kiss. My life was filled with possibility! Having dreams is a healthy thing. The Bible says, "Where there is no vision, the people perish."[2] We need dreams and goals because they offer us a vision to live by. They add purpose and create a passionate connection with life. Dreams propel us forward into the future. But the loss of these dreams can bring us to a stalemate, causing us to become resentful and blame God.

As a child I had the dream of becoming a professional football, basketball, or baseball player. I played every sport in high school and also played multiple sports in college. Athletics defined my childhood; my identity and purpose came from dreams of competing. Sports meant more to me than anything in the world. Being an athlete was all I had ever done—it was everything I knew. Then, one day, I graduated from college, and it was over. I went to a free-agent tryout for the Cleveland Browns and didn't get called back. Just like that, the dream was over. Something in me died that day. The passion that had made my heart beat was gone. I looked at the future and saw nothing.

I look back now and realize that I had no training or preparation to handle such a loss. My dreams were gone and I felt as if I'd lost everything. I went on to marry and have children. I worked a nine-to-five job and went through the motions. But inside, I felt like a failure. I experienced pain, depression, and anxiety as I searched desperately for something to replace my dream. Filled with inner resentment and anger, I looked for a way to medicate my pain. And eventually, this became an addiction.

After the death of my dream, I became resentful toward life, God, and ultimately myself. I thought that perhaps if I had taken better care of myself or had been better prepared, I could have lived my dream. But it didn't happen, and I was furious with myself for failing. Eventually, I turned the anger inward and suffered from depression and isolation. I continued to chase crazy opportunities, trying to resurrect my dead dreams. When those didn't work out, I fell even deeper into despair. My discontent affected everything, and my marriage ended in divorce.

Most of us are taught to pursue dreams, but few of us learn how to cope with their loss. Yet most of us will hold tight to dreams that don't come true. Even though we pursue and strive for them, we often fall short of seeing the dream fulfilled. How we respond to this loss will have huge implications on the quality of our lives. It's essential that we learn how to move on when life doesn't turn out the way we had planned. My inability to understand the loss of my dream cost me almost twenty years of my life. I faced depression, addictions, and divorce—all because I was ill-prepared for dealing with the loss of my hopes and dreams. I never processed the losses. I never discussed them with a trusted friend. I struggled in silence.

Psychologist and author, Larry Crabb, discusses loss in his book, *Shattered Dreams*. He says if we're not careful we'll make our dreams into idols.[3] When dreams, rather than God, give our lives meaning and purpose, they have taken on idol status. But the significance we long for can only come from God. Now don't get me wrong—God wants us to pursue our dreams and visions. But they must be rooted in His purpose. The key to fulfilling our dreams is to pursue God first. With His healthy perspective of our vision, God will use our pursuit to grow us into the men and women He plans for us to be.

I watched my youngest son also dream of becoming a great athlete. We, as a family, shared in the dream with him. We imagined watching him play in college, as we sat in the stands on a Saturday afternoon being part of the pageantry. Then, in his junior year of high school, he broke his back. We discovered he had defective vertebrae, and his dream ended. We all shared in the loss of that dream.

We will all experience dreams that do not come true. I have a good friend who moved to Nashville to become a singer, and it didn't happen for her. She has been struggling with the loss of that dream for ten years now, even though she has long since moved on professionally. It's important to grieve these losses so that God can bring about new dreams. When I got married, I had blissful dreams that I would be happy forever. But I wasn't. Marriage didn't empty the half-full glass of grief that I brought into the marriage. I now realize I had grandiose ideas about marriage. I thought it would be the catalyst to take away my pain, but this myth only set me up for more loss.

In *From Hurt to Hope*, the authors discuss this problem of not being taught how to deal with loss. Author Farah Moore shares, "I was not taught how to process loss. Consequently, I was oblivious to a need to teach that to my children. Losing my doll, watching my quarter roll into a street drain, watching my dad drive away without me, ripping my new coat, my best friend moving away, the death of my grandma, being very sick, not making the team, striking out, dropping the pass, losing an election, feeling left out or ignored, being misunderstood or ridiculed, the divorce of my parents, abuse, injury, rejection—our list can go on and on. The loss just kept happening."[4]

Betty Jo's Story

"The year I retired from teaching, my husband, Dan, had an episode with his heart that frightened us. He'd had a heart attack thirteen years prior, and as a rescue of that first heart attack he'd given his life to Christ. Through this first heart attack, we discovered an urgency we hadn't experienced. Suddenly we knew life was short. My husband understood he was going to die one day, but we certainly weren't prepared for what was about to happen.

"On a long Memorial Day weekend, we'd traveled to Memphis to relax and have some fun, and it was during this trip that my husband realized he was having another heart attack. We rushed to the hospital where they did a heart catharization. We knew he had some problems with his heart, but we'd always been told it wasn't life threatening. We weren't prepared to hear that this heart attack was severe.

"Eventually, we were able to leave the hospital and come home. Dan reminded me that we'd had thirteen years as a gift since the first heart attack. I told him that I wanted more. He kind of smiled and said, 'Well, I do too, but if we don't get it, you can't fall to pieces.' Some people have said Dan knew he was dying, but I don't think he did because we were up just an hour before he died—we both had gotten up to go to the restroom—and we didn't really talk. We just got up and went right back to bed. An hour later he woke me up when his heart stopped, causing him to have a seizure.

"From that moment on, it seemed as if I was walking in a dream. I knew when I got him off the bed that he was gone. When we got to the hospital, they immediately carried me to the quiet room. As soon as they said the "quiet room," I knew what they were preparing me for. I don't remember much about the doctor—I remember she was very kind when she came in to tell me that Dan had died. It just seemed like I was not a part of the whole experience at all, like God had taken me to another place to keep me calm and strong for the days ahead. I remember the people that were around me—my family—but I don't remember many details. I felt removed from it at times, but I remember that the sweetest thing that came out of that experience was God's grace. I've always believed in God's grace, but suddenly I had experienced it. It became real to me.

"At the funeral home, there would be times when I felt totally and completely wiped out, as if I was about to collapse. I felt like I'd cried every tear I could cry and my body was weak and tired, but then I would feel this supernatural strength that encompassed my whole body and held me up. I told my girls, 'I know what God's grace is all about. He is here with me. He's giving it to me.' I alternated between feeling His grace and power, believing I would be okay, and then feeling the extreme weakness again. But repeatedly, it was as if God's power enabled me to stand when physically I was totally worn out. Then a peace, as the Bible says, that passes all understanding came over me. I imagined someone standing there with me—it was a feeling that energized my body, empowering me to walk through that experience. God became real to me like never before, and it was confirmation that the grace of God that I'd always read about is really an awesome thing."

LOSS OF INNOCENCE

When we are children, we are like pristine lakes. Throughout life, ships run aground and spill oil and sludge throughout the lake, eventually killing the fish and birds. The black oil has contaminated the once beautiful water, rocks, and shores. Contamination may come in the form of physical, spiritual, or emotional abuse. Usually there's some tragic or troubling event, such as a divorce, that wounds the childlike spirit. For some, these wounds never heal.

At Restore Ministries, most of the people we work with have had some kind of experience as a child that deeply wounded them emotionally and spiritually. They come as adults struggling with issues that can almost always be traced back to an event in their childhoods. Trauma doesn't have to come from a single moment. It can result from a parent who tells you repeatedly that you'll never amount to anything. It can come from the fear of living in an unstable home. Perhaps you were touched inappropriately, or you were expected to provide emotional support for an adult. Maybe you were simply never told that you were loved and valued. Or maybe you had to make a significant move and were unable to settle into your new environment. All of these are tragic childhood losses.

The loss of innocence can be one of the more difficult losses to grieve, because we frequently cover up this sort of loss. We may self-medicate to soothe the trauma, ultimately leading us to addictions that reach a level of destructiveness. When we delve into the problem, more often than not we realize that childhood trauma is the source of these addictions.

LOSS OF A LOVED ONE

Perhaps the greatest loss of all is the loss of a loved one. In my life, I have been dealing with my mother's Alzheimer's. Although she is still living, Alzheimer's has taken her mind—the part that I loved so much and was able to connect with. Recently I was in the grocery store smelling Brute aftershave when John Denver's song, "Back Home Again," came on the radio. My dad loved this song because it reminded him of my mother. And I began to weep there in the middle of the aisle as I was reminded that my mother will never again ask me how I'm doing. She will never play cards with me or cook another meal for me. She doesn't recognize her grandchildren. I look at the picture of my parents on the bookshelf in my office and I understand the fullness of this loss.

The last time I visited my mother in the nursing home, she didn't even know I was her son. I became angry with how life was treating her. How could this sweet, loving woman have this happen to her? I left there in near disbelief. I think that's a common response for many of us when people we love are taken from us. Inside we scream, "No way! It can't be true! This isn't happening to me!"

The loss of a loved one is a pain that never completely fades, but it can heal. We can find peace in the midst of our loss. This is the hope we find in Christ: "If our hope in Christ is for this life only, we should be pitied more than anyone else in the world. But Christ has truly been raised from the dead—the first one and proof that those who sleep in death will also be raised" (1 Cor. 15:19–20 NCV).

LOSS OF PLACE

When I was about thirty-five, I visited my childhood home and took a long walk through town. The basketball court was still there, the public school, the recreation center, the bowling alley, the shopping mall, both of my grandparents' houses, the little market where my dad took me to get some pop and chips—it was all right there within walking distance. This had been my childhood. This old WWII-style neighborhood where all the houses were the same and most of the residents were WWII vets. There was no air-conditioning, so everyone would sit on their porches with citronella candles burning to keep the bugs away. We'd listen to the Cleveland Indians and Cincinnati Reds on the radio. Our hometown wasn't a far cry from Mayberry.

There's a scene near the end of the movie *Camelot* where Arthur sings a song, mourning the end of an era: "That once there was a spot / For one brief shining moment that was known as Camelot."[5] That song could have been sung about my childhood. When I turned fourteen, we moved away. I lost my Camelot, my sheltered world, and it will never be again. To this day, I feel the loss. Whenever I'm having a bad day, feeling a little melancholy or somber, I think back and remember what it was like growing up in that little town. And while I sometimes wish I could go back, we all know that in life, nothing remains the same. All things must eventually change. We get older and we begin to take on responsibility. We all must grow up.

LOSS OF LOVE

The dreams and expectations we have for our lives often parallel our dreams for love and marriage. And when a marriage ends, the loss of the dream traumatizes every member of the family—not just the couple involved. It's a pain that's hard to accept.

In some ways, marriage can be compared to a new pair of shoes. When you first buy the shoes, you can't take your eyes off them. You put them on your feet and check them out—they're just so cool. And it actually takes some time for them to get broken in; you might get a few blisters before they stretch to fit just right, but you're willing to go through the pain because you simply adore them. As the years go by, though, they become less shiny and no longer have the illusion of perfection. It's easy to disregard how comfortable they are compared to when they were new. They no longer create that mood-altering affect, and you start to see them as simply something to keep your feet dry.

What we want, what we expect, what we hope to have in life is often very different from what God has planned for us. I wanted to believe that I would marry a wonderful woman and live a passionate, happy existence with our perfect kids. But my life didn't follow the blueprint I had drawn up in my head, and I ended up divorced. As the venerable Harry Emerson Fosdick wrote, "Very few persons have a chance to live their lives on the basis of their first choice. We all have to live upon the basis of our second and third choices."[6] This is hard for most of us to accept. We aren't willing to live with second or even third choices. In America, that's considered failure. But we need to come to grips with this reality and understand that no loss is too great to overcome.

For many people, marital expectations do not materialize. There is an idealistic hope of what marriage is going to be, and it doesn't match up to reality. The reality is that marriage involves two imperfect, flawed people attempting to connect. It can be messy and difficult. It can disappoint at times, and it takes work, communication, commitment, and intimacy. We inevitably find that no person, no relationship has the power to give us the significance and purpose that can only come from God. The responsibility for making our marriages successful lies in the work we do individually with God because when we're growing spiritually, we have so much more to offer a partner.

LOSS OF SUCCESS

When we try something new and fail to accomplish our goal, we experience a loss. The greater our desire for something, the greater the risk that we will be hurt if we don't get it. Sometimes people desire something so much that they will not risk the hurt of failure and just won't try at all. It is inevitable that we are going to fail at some things we attempt in life, and with failure comes a sense of loss.

We need to work through losses because if we close our hearts due to painful failures, we stop living the adventure of life. Life is sometimes like a game of dodgeball. You can continue to dodge situations that have the potential for loss, or you can stand there and try to catch the ball. If you drop the ball, you lose, but if you keep it, you have victory. In other words, you have to deal with the risk and not allow the fear of loss or failure to stop you.

Let's look at the life of a person who had significant losses in his life but never gave up: Abraham Lincoln.

He failed in business at age 21.

He was defeated in a legislative race at age 22.

He failed again in business at age 24.

He experienced the death of his sweetheart at age 26.

He had a nervous breakdown at age 27.

He lost a congressional race at age 34.

He lost another congressional race at age 36.

He lost a senatorial race at age 45.

He failed in an effort to become Vice President at age 47.

He lost another senatorial race at age 47.

He was elected President of the United States at age 52.

Obviously, Lincoln worked through his losses and continued to move forward, accepting new possibilities and new challenges. He persevered. Had he not, our country might have been forever changed for the worse. In the face of such challenges, many of us would probably have retreated and given up. But Lincoln's faith in God was a driving force. He believed in the abilities God gave him, no matter what the circumstances told him. And so he persevered.

My dad was a high school basketball coach. I remember the year his team won the regional championship. They were excited about going on to the state championship. But once there, they didn't advance—they got beat by a rival school in the first game. It devastated my dad, but he had the ability to bounce back each year for a new season. He was resilient. He knew how to put the loss into perspective and learn from it.

It was a huge loss for me when college ended and my athletic career was over. I later went through a painful divorce, and then my kids grew up and moved out on their own. I tried a couple of business ventures, and they failed. I'm fifty-two now, and I can't physically do all the things I once could—recently I had to give up playing basketball because of my back and I've also lost my hair. It may seem silly, but I miss the feeling of the wind blowing in my hair, of a comb going through it. It's over—I'll never have that feeling again. I'm losing my youth—quickly—and all that comes with it.

These are all legitimate losses, and sometimes these losses make me feel defeated, as if life has played a big trick on me. But reading about Abraham Lincoln and thinking about my dad makes me desire resilience. I have moved on to greater possibilities. I'm coming to realize that my life hasn't been a complete failure. It's as Henri Nouwen once wrote: "We find new courage to let new things happen, things over which we have no control.... And it is here that we find courage to face our human boundaries and hurts, whether our physical appearance, our being excluded by others, our memories of hurt or abuse, our oppression at the hands of another."[7]

I was in denial for years that my athletic career was over at the college level. I couldn't accept it. I was always scheming for some way, some team, or some sport that might come along and resurrect my dream. I even became a boxer, and then I tried golf. I wanted to become a pro bowler. Of course my efforts were sad and futile attempts to feel loved through my ability in sports. And my refusal to accept my failed dreams had me chasing illusions. I caused those I loved a great deal of pain when I should have moved on with my life and accepted reality.

Many of the people who seek help at Restore Ministries are chasing dreams they'll never see, dreams that were over before they even started.

But they can't seem to let go of them, so they remain trapped in a cycle of grief for years. They aren't able to embrace a new beginning, and they miss being fully alive in the present.

When I began recovery in 1997, my heart had finally broken open, and God began pouring His Holy Spirit into my emptiness. He healed my losses and walked me through this period of grief. That's when my recovery truly began.

REFLECTION QUESTIONS

What is a significant loss that you experienced in your childhood? How did you feel about it then and how do you feel about it now?

Make a list of losses you have experienced in your life, no matter how small or great. Be as honest as possible.

Which of these losses listed above are you still grieving? How have these losses influenced your life?

Have your dreams for marriage come true? If you haven't been married, how has that impacted your life? Do you consider it a loss or a failure on your part? If you are married, have your expectations of marriage been accurate?

How do you hope to heal by being a part of this study?

REFLECTIONS

REFLECTIONS

REFLECTIONS

REFLECTIONS

CHAPTER TWO

OVERCOMING THE ANGER ASSOCIATED WITH LOSS

The moment we begin to deal with our anger over a failed dream is when we've moved on from denial. Once we can no longer deny the loss, reality hits and we become angry. We ask ourselves—or we ask God—"Why did this have to happen to me? This just isn't fair." When our dreams are thwarted, we might feel that fate or God has somehow robbed us. And yet God always has a better plan than we can comprehend for each of us. Failing or losing a dream might be the catalyst for you finally turning your dreams over to Him. God can pick up the leftovers of a broken plan and turn them into something beautiful. Instead of resenting God's change of plans, go with it! When you can't see God's hand, trust God's heart.

When we harbor resentment, we stay stuck in anger—sometimes for decades—unable or unwilling to move on. I often counsel men who don't get the promotions they feel they deserve. When the reality finally sets in that they've been passed over, their anger is sometimes explosive. Life seems unfair to them. It takes them a while to realize God has a different plan, a better plan, and that they need to trust Him to carry it out in their lives. Disappointment will abound in life, but learning how to respond to it in a healthy way is the key to resolving anger.

Often our expectations coincide with a sense of entitlement. We think God should bless us and give us what we want. This is a dangerous line of thought. When we start feeling entitled, it's natural to become angry when those expectations are not met. We need someone to blame, and sometimes we blame ourselves. At Restore Ministries, I encounter people who are angry with their spouses, their employers, the government, you name it. But many times, they're ultimately angry with God. But most of this anger can be traced to a sense of entitlement: *I deserve the best. I want my first choice.* But chasing elusive dreams can mean that we miss the best choice—God's choice for us.

Those who remain bitter and resentful often engage in addictive behaviors. They medicate their anger by eating or substance abuse. They have multiple affairs and commit inappropriate sexual acts. Ultimately, an angry person will do whatever it takes to stifle the burning anger they feel inside. The relapse acronym we use in recovery is HALT: Hungry, Angry, Lonely, and Tired. These are the states in which an addict is most susceptible to relapse. Anger, the word for second letter, is a sure path to addiction relapse. One of my best methods for dealing with anger is to read Scripture. The 23rd Psalm always reminds me that the Lord is with me, providing everything that I truly need: peace, serenity, time alone, or simply His companionship. He will provide and be there for me.

> The LORD is my shepherd; I have everything I need.
> He lets me rest in green meadows; he leads me beside peaceful streams.
> He renews my strength.
> He guides me along right paths, bringing honor to his name.
> Even when I walk through the darkest valley,
> I will not be afraid, for you are close beside me.
> Your rod and your staff protect and comfort me.
> You prepare a feast for me in the presence of my enemies,
> You honor me by anointing my head with oil.

My cup overflows with blessings.
Surely your goodness and unfailing love will pursue me all the days
    of my life,
And I will live in the house of the LORD forever. (NLT)

God makes it clear who we are to be dependent upon in our crisis. The psalmist says, "The LORD is my Shepherd, I have all that I need." Think about a time when you have wanted something intensely and it didn't work out. How did it make you feel? Those times can be extremely stressful, and can lead to a sense of anger and resentment against whomever or whatever. But this psalm brings about a sense of peace and serenity. It reminds us that if we let go of our anger and trust in God, then He will take care of us.

HAVING THE WRONG EXPECTATIONS

In one of our Restore Ministries groups, we were discussing expectations—how we often expect too much from people and essentially let ourselves down when they don't act the way we expect them to act. I expect my wife to be there for me and love me for the rest of my life. There's nothing wrong with that expectation, except that anything could happen to dash that hope. She could, heaven forbid, be killed in car accident tonight coming home. There are things in life that we simply can't control and nothing is guaranteed to us. And if that terrible thing happened, I would have to make a choice whether to be angry or to move past the anger and to embrace the feelings that come along with the loss of the expectation that my wife would be around for me to love for the rest of my life. We cannot control many of our circumstances, but we can control where we place our faith. We can put our faith and hope in Christ, trusting that He will take care of us even in the midst of our loss and pain.

The longer I live, the more I understand that there are no guarantees in life. If I want to live in this world and be at peace, open to new experiences and ideas, then I have to learn to really believe the words of the 23rd Psalm. I must place my life in Christ's hands and trust Him.

Another great example of this in the Bible is the story of Nebuchadnezzar, Meshach, Shadrach, and Abednego (Daniel 3). King Nebuchadnezzar has plans to throw Meshach, Shadrach, and Abednego in the furnace because of their lack of loyalty to the King. But as they're cranking up the furnace, and King Nebuchadnezzar is applying pressure to make these three bow down to him as king and praise his name instead of the Lord's, their response is profound: "You know what, Nebuchadnezzar? Our God can deliver us from this; He's that powerful. But even if He doesn't—we're not bowing down to you" (v. 16). That is the healthy perspective toward God and this world that we need to have. We have to say, "You know what? He's in control of my life, and if He wants to give me something, He will. But if He chooses not to, I'm still going to trust Him." Proverbs 3:5–6 echoes this idea, "Trust the Lord with all your heart, and don't depend on your own understanding. Remember the LORD in all you do, and he will give you success" (NCV).

Betty Jo's Story

"My anger did not come in the beginning. It happened the year following my husband's death. I had some severe back problems, and even before my husband died I knew I needed surgery because we'd exhausted all other options. I made the decision to go ahead with the surgery a year after my husband died, but it did not go well. I didn't realize I was still in the grieving process, and I believe this contributed to the difficulty my body had in healing. A staph infection developed in my spine, so I had to have a series of surgeries. I had some complications with some of the metal penetrating internally in my body. After about the third surgery, I began to have a lot of discontentment in my spirit.

"I wouldn't allow myself to think that I could possibly be angry with God. But it had gotten so bad that I would go to church and receive nothing from the service. I could tell that my spirit was not where it needed to be. I was praying, I was reading my Bible, but things weren't going right. I remember talking with my pastor who gave me some great insight into the grieving process. As I sat across from him, he kindly asked, 'Do you think you could be just a little bit angry about losing Dan and your health?' I hadn't been able to work, and so at that time I was concerned about having to quit work. And when he said that, I remember saying, 'How could I ever be angry at God? He's been so good to me throughout this whole process.' And he said, 'We can say we're not angry, but if we are, God knows it. And anger doesn't just disappear because you say you're not angry.' His question caused me to do some probing, and on my way home that day, I began to bawl. I cried the same kind of tears I did when I first lost Dan. And I remember telling God that I didn't want to be angry, that I knew He'd been so powerfully good to me. It was almost like I was afraid to be angry with God. I told God, 'But I don't want to feel this way.' When I voiced this, I felt peace—it was an assurance that everything was going to be okay.

"I had to go through the anger. I see that now. But back then, I had to recognize that I wasn't accepting it. Maybe you are at this point in your walk through grief. It's okay to express your anger. You will discover a peace that passes all understanding (Phil. 4:7)."

RESENTMENT

Resentment is a simmering anger—an anger you keep returning to like a clean pig returns to the mud. If we aren't able to forgive, resentment can lead us into addictive behavior. Resentment breeds self-pity, and self-pity causes us to try to medicate the anger—this is how the addiction cycle begins. With chronic resentment, we often turn our anger inward and it develops into depression.

I had a friend who kept getting passed over for job promotions, year after year. He was angry and eventually he became depressed. He resented himself and felt like a failure. This was the pattern I followed as well. My dreams and goals didn't work out the way I had planned, so I simmered in chronic resentment toward myself, my life, my God, and the people who I selfishly asked to bail me out of my mess. I hurt the people who loved me and I made a mess of my life. Looking back, I can now see the pattern of formation for my own addictions: I didn't get what I wanted, and I was mad at myself for not achieving it. I blamed myself, and then I took it out on everybody else.

When we perpetuate anger by refusing to forgive, it turns into resentment. We might hate a spouse for divorcing us, resent an employer who passes us over, or be angry with a teacher or coach who told us we were worthless. Some of us even feel angry with loved ones who die. And at the heart of most resentment is anger toward God. We blame Him for not giving us the life we wanted and expected.

We see this in people who come to Restore Ministries. A Restore intern told me recently about a loss in her life:

> When I was a girl I had a deeply ingrained idea that one day the perfect man would come into my life and sweep me off my feet, and that romance would be the thing to save me from reality. Perfect joy and bliss would be mine when I met the stranger who would see beauty in me and be, essentially, my Christ. I found, as I got older, that it was very difficult to find a perfect man—or even a good one. Men who were given over to Christ were scarce, and even those were deeply flawed—nothing like the prince I'd been waiting for. I recently broke up with a guy and saw my dreams for relationships finally crushed. I could see very clearly that men were always going to fail me on one level or another, and I was

angry at all of them for some time. Then I was angry at God for a while longer. How could He have put us here on Earth merely to disappoint? It didn't matter that I knew it was to bring me closer to Him and show me my dependence on Him. Still, the pain was acute and I resented God. One day, someone reminded me of the way God likes to replace dreams. He delights in bringing new and better dreams to replace the old. I know this now. I see how much better His dreams are than mine.

As humans, we are notorious for punishing ourselves with regret. *What if I had married someone else? What if I had finished college? What if I would have been in a different place at a different time?* We will always feel the need to blame someone or something when we are in denial. We can scrutinize situations and decisions for years, but it won't change the past. Instead, it empowers us to remain a victim. Eventually our anger turns inward, and we resent ourselves for being so stupid. In *Voice of the Heart*, author Chip Dodd writes, "Avoiding hurt renders us numb and, therefore, numbs our hearts and their hunger for healing and life which comes through relationships."[1] It is much easier to hold onto resentment and blame someone or something else for the hurt than it is for us to take responsibility for our own pain. Resentment seems like the easy road that most of us take rather than dealing with our hurts, loss, and disappointment.

As I've already mentioned, one of the dangers of resentment is that it leads to self-pity. When I began my personal recovery, one of the underlying causes for the poor choices I was making was depression. My dreams had ended with no possibility of being resurrected. The day I graduated from college, that cold truth hit me. Writing about it is still painful, but resentment is no longer eating away at my life.

Over the years, my refusal to deal with this disappointment eventually led me into several addictive responses. I began to see that I was angry at the world. I didn't get what I wanted, my dreams were not fulfilled, but more important, I deeply resented myself. I suffered from the "could-have/should-have/if-only" syndrome. The past ate away at me, and resentment was destroying me. I could not connect to the present reality. I wanted to escape. In my spirit I was numb. I had no relationship with God, and all of my other relationships were very one-sided. I was so angry with the way things had turned out, and I let that anger control other areas of my life. Anger led to addictions and turned inward to depression.

Anger can be a healthy, natural emotion. But when anger becomes a chronic resentment or bitterness, we stay stuck in this phase of the grieving process. Until we can move to the next stage, we cannot conquer our grief and begin to grow.

And so, my resentment remained and stunted my growth. I stayed in the same place emotionally and spiritually, still addicted and depressed. I had turned my anger inward, particularly during the decline and eventual death of my mother. When someone we so closely associate with our own joy and happiness has died, it makes us angry. I remember asking God, "Why does life have to be so painful? I want my mother back! I don't want life to end this way."

Yet, as we've said before, life is about loss. We cannot go back or change things that have happened. Instead, we need to adopt the attitude of the apostle Paul, who said, "I know that I have not yet reached that goal, but there is one thing I always do. Forgetting the past and straining toward what is ahead" (Phil. 3:13 NCV).

REFLECTION QUESTIONS

If you could ask God why something specific has happened in your life, what event or situation would you ask Him about?

What one thing in your life do you regret more than anything else?

What would you change about the past if you could?

If God were to ask you, "What are you so mad about?" what would your response be?

Are you harboring resentment toward someone or something? Explain. In your anger over loss, who are you angry with: God, yourself, someone else, or all of the above? Explain.

REFLECTIONS

REFLECTIONS

CHAPTER THREE

BARGAINING

*"And remind me Lord, when I can't hold on any longer,
that terrifying being who wrestled with Jacob in the
dark turned out to be, in dawn, an angel . . . an angel
who had the power to bestow on him a blessing."*
—ANONYMOUS

In Minirth and Meier's *Love is a Choice Workbook*, *bargaining* is described as "the tricks that we use to try to hustle ourselves out of a bad situation. Who has not, in desperation, tried to bargain with God by saying, 'God, if only you'll get me out of this mess, I'll . . . ?' We use bargains to try to get an edge against our pain, so that we can go around it instead of through it."[1] Through our wishing or thinking, we try to manipulate, hustle, or squirm our way out of or into something. In an effort to avoid the pain in grief and loss, we bargain with God, others, and even ourselves. The goal is to bargain our way *around*—instead of going *through*—the pain or suffering that comes with loss. But avoidance causes us to go in a circle, and we end up in the exact place we started.

I can remember many times promising to serve God for the rest of my life if he would only let me become a professional football player. I vowed to do anything He asked, as long as He would let me live my dream. This bargaining began when my dream was first conceived, and

I kept it up long after the dream had actually ended. I bargained with God because I didn't want to deal with the loss and pain. It was my way of keeping the dream—or the illusion of it—alive.

Greg, a man I counseled at Restore Ministries, is a perfect example of this. Greg was referred to us by his church. He'd recently separated from his wife due to an addiction to pornography. Greg was not unlike many of the men I work with who have ruined their marriages because of addictions—he bargained. Once reality set in and his marriage had already disintegrated, he suddenly make a conversion to be a faithful Christian, believing it would save his marriage. And while many men do make sincere efforts to change, others throw around empty promises, saying things like, "I promise I'll never do it again. God has shown me the error of my ways. He's forgiven me; you should too." The most obvious offenders will say, "I will change as long as you stay and give me a second chance." This is a classic case of bargaining to get out of a bad situation. The panic of facing immense pain and heartache sets in, and instead of dealing with the consequences of our actions, we want a quick fix to get our lives back on track.

BARGAINING WITH GOD

A big part of this bargaining game involves God. When husbands delve into pornography and cause marriages to crumble, they might bargain with God to step in and save the marriages. Again, they use if/then statements: "If you save my marriage, then I'll start going to church." Or, they might appeal to God's design for marriage: "God, I know you hate divorce, so save my marriage. Make it work out." But there is no bargaining with God. Bargaining rarely works with their spouses either. Both God and wives recognize these words for what they are: empty promises with no intention of change.

These husbands come to us at Restore Ministries because they want out of the pain. They are scared of the consequences of their actions, and they are grieving what they have done. Of course this happens with women as well. They might find themselves caught up in an affair or some other marriage-ending problem. When the husband discovers the affair, she is faced with the task of saving her marriage, trying to get the husband to stay. What I teach men and women is that they cannot control their spouses' reactions. Nor can they manipulate God. Each of us must accept responsibility for our actions, deeds, and addictions and then accept the consequences and go through the grief.

In reality, God wants our marriages to work even more than we do. He also wants to grow us into men and women of honor, into people who love Him with our whole hearts. He doesn't want to be a form of escape for our problems. He is more concerned with our hearts than our circumstances. We have to come to grips with the fact that God may choose not to change our circumstances, but He will use circumstances to change us. If we attempt to bargain our way out of pain, we lose the opportunity to grow through it. If we choose to bypass pain and move onto something else, we will miss what God wants to teach us—and we'll repeat the cycle of denial and anger.

We must own a genuine sense of responsibility and approach God with an "I will allow You to change me" attitude. This is not a conditional *if*. It's an authentic response. We must be able to honestly say, "If it takes the shattering of my dream for my character to be developed, then don't let me avoid the pain." We can't manipulate God. God does not respond to *ifs*.

There is a prayer about pain and suffering that I keep in my Bible to share with recovery groups: "Lord, help me to understand the nature and purpose of pain. Chisel away everything that is not of you, until you are formed in me. Give me the strength to hold on to that which now may seem most painful, but in the end will turn out to be that which best serves my soul. And remind me Lord, when I can't hold on any longer, that the terrifying being who wrestled with Jacob in the dark turned out to be, in dawn, an angel . . . an angel who had the power to bestow on him a blessing" (author unknown).

I think one of the problems with loss is that we often can't see how anything good could possibly come from the experience. There tends to be a darkness around us that conceals any ray of light. And yet, the Bible reminds us in Romans 8:28 that the good is out there, even when we can't see it: "We know that in everything God works for the good of those who love him" (NCV).

In the midst of pain, it's hard to see how loosing something meaningful can possibly best serve our soul. Yet God has promised He will use it for good. Believing in the goodness of God when we are suffering is one of the hardest things we humans will ever do. When we are grieving a loss, being able to wait in the hope of Christ is key.

Perhaps the greatest principle I've learned in recovery is patience. Patience requires nothing more of me than to sit still and wait. This is what I love about the story of the parting of the Red Sea. The children of Israel had the Red Sea in front of them and Pharaoh and his army at their backs. In their panic Moses told them, "Don't be afraid! Stand still and you will see the LORD save you today. You will never see these Egyptians again after today. You only need to remain calm; the LORD will fight for you" (Ex. 14:13–14 NCV).

Maybe you have a brick wall in front of you and regret at your back. Maybe you feel like there's no way you can move forward. Then stand still! You can be in a painful place but still experience the joy and comfort of Christ. The children of Israel had to trust that God was going to deliver them. When they were at their greatest need, God made a way through the Red Sea. He parted the waters, and they went through. Maybe you need to trust God to deliver you from your own Red Sea. Just as there was no way for the Israelites to go around the sea or around Pharaoh, there's no way to go around grief—you must go through it, and it will take God's help. As you go through trials, know God is making a way. If you try to avoid them or bargain your way out, you might miss the greatest blessing—the transformation of your character.

Betty Jo's Story

"I sometimes felt drawn back to the bedroom where I actually did the CPR and tried to help Dan. That's where I believe he died, even though they pronounced him dead at the hospital. But it would seem as if I was being drawn back to that spot when I would pray. I remember one night praying and asking God to help me, because it seemed like everything about my life had changed. I wanted to feel better. I felt God was so present at that time and so close. I remember crying and begging God to let it be a dream. Just hearing myself say those words made me afraid I was going crazy. I knew it was real, but I was asking God to make it go away. I even said, 'You wept for Mary and Martha, so don't you feel bad for me? Don't you care about me?' When I said that, it convicted my heart. I knew He loved me, and I knew He was watching over me, but I was just so desperate for help. When you reach those stages, you have to let the grief out before you start getting better. After that, I didn't have any more of those episodes.

"There's no doubt that God is real. I always knew He was, but we don't really believe until we've tested it, until we've tasted and felt it through experience."

BARGAINING WITH OURSELVES AND WITH OUR LIVES

Just as we bargain with a spouse or with God, we also bargain with ourselves. We tell ourselves that we are going to do this or that or that we will never make the same mistake again. It's very much the same as when we try to manipulate or bargain our way out of dealing with reality. I worked with an alcoholic once who had lost his job, then lost his driver's license, and then landed in jail. He told himself he would never drink again. He vowed to work out and take care of his body. He said was going to start attending church. He gave himself high expectations—and they were great goals to strive for. But he tried to convince himself that change would take place overnight—a process that takes baby steps.

For years I believed that if my children were athletes, my failure to be a great athlete would resolve itself. So I spent the second half of my life bargaining on behalf of my children, trying to live vicariously through their achievements. If my kids could make it as great athletes, then my life would possess significance. I would have succeeded through them. Friends often told me to stop putting pressure on my kids, to let go of them. But I didn't let up because I couldn't deal with my own dreams being over. It's hard now to even admit this, but when I got into recovery, God helped me understand what I was doing. I finally started dealing with the loss of my childhood dreams.

Even if we are able to achieve our childhood dreams, one day they will come to an end. I can't count the number of times I've seen a successful athlete, who has achieved the dream, reluctantly retire. With cameras flashing, the athlete cries tears of joy and appreciation for an amazing career—but there are also tears of loss, because the dream has ended. They will never run those fields of glory again. They will grieve because that chapter of their lives is over. It's not easy to let go and deal with the pain of this loss.

We can take this feeling of grief and loss and bargaining with life to a place of internal shame and again, regret. We become victim to the "if only's": "If only I'd been a better father." "If only I'd been skinnier, he wouldn't have left me." "If only I had been more successful, I would be loved by my colleagues." Instead of grieving and accepting the paths we've traveled, we wallow in the "if only's." We feel stupid for letting these things happen. It becomes toxic shame that renders us unable to grieve and move forward. To wallow in shame is almost as damaging as the loss of the dreams themselves. We have to become open and vulnerable to the pain in order to move forward to healing and recovery.

REFLECTION QUESTIONS

How are you bargaining to avoid the pain of a significant loss?

What deals have you made with God or others recently? In what ways are you keeping up with your "end of the bargain"?

How have you bargained with God to get what you wanted in the past? How have you bargained with yourself? How have you bargained with others?

If pain is the chisel that shapes our character, is there a painful situation you're trying to avoid that God may be using to develop your character?

Can you point to a painful situation in your life that God used to build your character?

REFLECTIONS

REFLECTIONS

REFLECTIONS

REFLECTIONS

CHAPTER FOUR

DEPRESSION AND SADNESS

When things don't turn out the way we had hoped, or when we face divorce, death, loss of employment, an illness, or some other loss, we are susceptible to falling into depression. When we don't address the anger we experience after a loss, sometimes we become numb to the pain. We lose our drive to get up and get out of bed. Life becomes gray. We don't feel anything—we don't *want* to feel anything. Things that used to bring joy and excitement no longer stir our hearts or sensibilities.

The stages of grief are not five fluid steps that you can go through in precise order and then "graduate" from your grief. It's possible that you may move forward to a stage, only to regress back into a previous stage. For some, the process of grieving a loss may take the rest of their lives. Something might happen to trigger memories that cause us to slip back into an earlier stage of grief. But as time goes by we're able to move through the grieving process and experience new hope. Just as an addict can have a relapse, we can also experience relapses in our grief recovery. It's important to know that these relapses are temporary—they don't have to lead to permanent depression. Sometimes I experience periods when I am sad about what I missed as my children were growing up. I missed some great times and important events because of my addictions. It makes me angry at myself, and if I allow myself to feel anger long enough, it makes me depressed as well. Missing those precious times was a consequence of my addictions and divorce. Today, I have moved on to acceptance, but there are times when I still get very sad about it. I still grieve that loss and continue to heal from it, and I probably will for the rest of my life. God has healed me and transformed me, but I know that I can never get back what I have lost with them.

I have healthy relationships with my adult children now, but their childhood is gone. Every year I experience some regret over the things I missed, but I remind myself that they're grown now and childhood is over. Some nights I walk by their now empty rooms and feel the loss. It seems that only yesterday they were filled with little voices.

Recently, I visited the street where I grew up from 1954 to 1969. I thought about the time when my parents were young and healthy. Part of me wished my childhood had never ended. I had great joy there, but it is gone. I don't know how many people have lived there since or how many kids have grown up on that street. It's been thirty-eight years, but as I stood there it felt like it was yesterday. Sadness washed over me because I miss my carefree childhood.

Sadness is a natural response to loss. Minirth and Meier have a great description of sadness in their *Love is a Choice Workbook:* "Sadness is the healthy means to relieving pain and loss. Sadness is ordinary. Sadness is the appropriate response to sad events. Best of all, sadness is not endless. Unlike chronic depression, repetition and suppressed anger, sadness comes, is recognized, and goes. This is when you settle down for a good, old-fashioned cry. You may want to cry alone, but at times you might find it very helpful to do your crying on a sympathetic shoulder. Give yourself time at this stage; don't look for any quick fixes. There's a lot of wisdom in the old saying, 'A good cry cleanses the soul.' Visualize your tears washing away your pain. And remember, God is always accessible. Let yourself be gathered into the comfort of His presence."[1]

In the movie, *City of Angels,* Nicholas Cage's character Seth hypothesizes about crying: "Maybe emotion becomes so intense your body just can't contain it. Your mind and your feelings become too powerful . . . and your body weeps."[2]

Betty Jo's Story

"After Dan's death, I experienced no pleasure. I remember staying up as late as possible because going to the bedroom brought back the realization that he was gone. I wanted to be so tired that I would fall asleep immediately, so I wouldn't have to think about it. I was going to bed at eleven-thirty or twelve o'clock, and I would get up at five-thirty in the morning. And I was starting the day and ending the day the same way. It was as if my life had changed. I remember asking my medical doctor, 'Is this the way it's always going to be?'

"There was no excitement, no joy about anything. Getting dressed, doing my hair—I remember changing clothes three or four times before I'd leave the house. I'd look in the mirror and finally say, "This is as good as it's going to get.' My face didn't even look the same. It was as if I was wearing my grief. It was overwhelming—I don't even know how to describe the gray sadness. I could be in a crowd with people around me all the time, but there was no spark to my life. It seemed like every day was the same. There were moments that were lighter than others, but for those first few months, I was just trying to make it through the day. I didn't want my kids to know that I felt that bad because I knew that they were mourning for their dad. It was the same loss for them, so I didn't want them to worry about me.

"But I thought about Dan all the time. He was my best friend. He was the only one who made me smile. I've learned since then that, no, that's not right, I can experience life again. But during this period in my life the sadness was so consuming that it took a while to get the joy, laughter and fun back into life."

THE DIFFERENCE BETWEEN DEPRESSION AND SADNESS

When we are angry in the grieving process, it is because we don't want what has happened to actually be true. In depression, we transfer the anger toward ourselves, turn it inward, and begin hating who we are. Everything becomes dull, and life loses its preciousness. When we're depressed, we don't want to feel or sometimes to even exist. But there is a difference between clinical depression and sadness. When we're sad, we're still feeling. We don't want to *dull* the pain; we want it to go away. We don't want to cease to be; we want to be happy. Dr. Dodd refers to sadness this way, "Sadness is the feeling that speaks to how much we value what is missed, what is gone, and what is lost. It also speaks of how deeply you value what you love, what you have, and what you live."[3] He goes on to explain that sadness is proportional—the more you value something the more it is going to hurt.

My oldest dog, Jackie, has been a constant, faithful companion since my recovery began. I love the way he brings his ball everywhere with him, the way he likes to snuggle up next to me in bed. He has been with me for almost ten years now. When he passes away, it will break this animal-lover's heart because he has brought me such great joy. I love the way Dodd puts it: "How much we feel sadness for something shows how much we value what we have lost." Dodd explained that when he dies he hopes everyone comes to his funeral and cries profusely. You see, those tears mean that people knew him, loved him, valued him, and will miss him.[4]

I believe there is a transition between depression and sadness that is a healthy transition. The process begins when we experience depression over our losses. We become angry, turn it inward, and feel life is not worth living. The transition comes when we move from that state into sadness, where life becomes worth living again, and we are able and willing to feel. There is sadness still, and we miss that which has been lost, that which was so meaningful. But we stop being angry and depressed. Dr. Dodd writes, "One of the gifts of sadness is that it is the first step of healing from loss. Sadness is fundamental to a full life because it opens up the door to healing."[5]

In all my experience with recovery and in all the books I've read on the subject, I have found no clear-cut method for moving out of depression into sadness. But I believe that one of the most helpful things you can do is communicate with someone. Talk about it. Begin to see this stage as necessary, that it signals the end of grief, and believe you will make it through. The more you talk about it, the more you will begin to heal. Again, I am not talking about chronic sadness or clinical depression, both of which require medical evaluation. We're discussing losses in life that submerge us into grief. We have to be willing to talk about these situational depressions, these intense feelings of sadness.

Each of us will deal with the stages of this process differently. For some, sadness may not be intense, but they might feel that way for longer. Others might experience brief, but tremendous, sadness. As you begin to float through bouts of sadness, you are nearing the final stage of grief, which is acceptance. When you finally move toward acceptance, you might still experience sadness. But it's an emotion you are willing to feel and perhaps even embrace. Once you can move through these stages and understand their benefits, they will move you toward healing, where you can focus on the finish line. If you can approach the sadness stage with honesty about the things you are missing, you will be able to expedite the grieving process. You can begin to experience memories with the sweetness and joy that they originally brought. You can sit back and remember the pleasure, and let the sadness of your heart honor those times.

When I look at my old house, I feel sadness because I remember things that I've lost. But I am so thankful for those times of my youth because they brought me such great pleasure. I have moved into acceptance that those days are gone, and there will be moments when I'll miss them, and I will be sad over those losses. But I want to live my life to the fullest, and I know that I must move past the loss of those dreams, past the pain, and honor them the way they deserve to be honored.

AGING

Many people get depressed as they get older. The moment we are born, we begin the death process. We have a finite existence. And although God is ageless and timeless, time on earth for humans is limited. For those who are seventy, eighty, or even ninety-years-old forward thinking is essential. Boredom and lack of purpose is fertile soil for depression. Bear Bryant predicted that he would die a year after he retired, and he did. Sometimes people that retire from life don't stay connected to the growth process.

We humans have a tendency to give up after a certain age. We begin to think there is nothing left for us to do in life. We've done the career thing, we've done the marriage thing, we've had kids, and we've traveled. Now we've become bored and lack purpose for the final stages of our lives. It sends us into a depressed state, and we don't know how to handle the loss of our youth.

In his book, *Personal Best*, Dr. Sheehan writes:

Remaining fresh, continuing to be creative—these options are always available to us whatever our age. We can have a rebirth, a resurrection, no matter how old we are in years. We must, however, accept responsibility for our lives, for our health. We must realize that living is an art, and life is an achievement. It is not a gift or a possession, it is our final battle.

How can one think that aging is a period to retire from life? It is quite the reverse. When all else are saying "you have earned this rest" we are filled with divine discontent. We have earned our spurs, we are warriors to reckon with. Yet friends and family would have us seek rest and resurrection. They would muster us out of the ranks of the militants and cause us to become spectators.[6]

We must always be in the process of growth until the day we die. Sue Monk Kidd writes in, *When the Heart Waits*, "That's the sacred intent of life, of God—to move us continuously toward growth, toward recovering all that is lost and orphaned within us and restoring the divine image imprinted on our soul."[7] The body ages, it is limited, it has a beginning and end date, but our spirit and our mind don't. They are ageless and eternal. We must always be engaged in the development of self. I realize at age fifty-two that I am superior to younger men, because my body has existed for these years. These are the most productive years of my life. I believe I am going to be smarter and wiser at eighty than I am now. There will be no retirement from life for me. I will not fade away and look back at life as a series of losses. Nobody is putting me out to pasture. I refuse to eat grass all day. I am going to live!

As he was writing *Personal Best*, Dr. Sheehan was fighting cancer. He writes about what it has taught him about the aging process and the death process:

> Death will not take me unawares. I expect now to be cut down in my prime, doing well at what I do best. Cancer has put urgency into my life. I, still unworthy, am about to return to my Creator. And I am learning something critically important about the human condition: No one, no matter their age, should ever retire from life.
>
> We must be forever enlarging our lives, not diminishing them. "Sin is closing the circle," wrote a contemporary theologian. Once we exclude anything or anybody we cease to grow. We join forces with sin and age and death.[8]

REFLECTION QUESTIONS

Have you experienced depression in your life? Have you experienced sadness? Describe the feelings that come with either or both.

When you are depressed or sad, what is life like for you?

Discuss any sadness you feel in your heart today.

How are you approaching the process of aging? What feelings are stirred when you think about getting older? Are you losing your passion and enthusiasm for life, or do you feel connected to a strong purpose?

Do you feel as if you are having a rebirth or resurrection at this time in your life?

REFLECTIONS

REFLECTIONS

REFLECTIONS

CHAPTER FIVE

FORGIVENESS

Forgiveness is extending grace where it might not necessarily be deserved. God has bestowed so much grace and mercy on us where we have not deserved it, and we are commanded to do the same. Ephesians 4:32 says, "Be kind and loving to each other, and forgive each other just as God forgave you in Christ" (NCV). The way we move through depression is by learning to accept what has happened and forgive those who played a role. Forgiving those who've hurt us, forgiving ourselves, and even forgiving God for the hurt and losses in our lives, frees us from depression and grief. It dissolves the anger toward the person or thing that has hurt us.

If you pour water on a fire in an outdoor pit, you'll notice that the water puts the fire out and smolders the coals. That is the same thing that happens when we forgive those that have hurt us: we eradicate the hot fire that has grown and, in the process, we let off a little steam. It is a release to allow the anger in our hearts to dissolve—this process is for our own benefit as much as for the benefit of others.

Christ tells us that forgiveness is for *us*, not for the person that has hurt us. If we forgive, we can live by the fruits of the Spirit. The central step in the process of moving to acceptance and coming to peace is forgiveness.

. is the cause of many chronic struggles for those who are
anger, withholding forgiveness. Whether we are angry at the
.ity figures that have wronged us, at our spouses who've not lived
.o our expectations, at our children for drifting away from us, or at
sickness that has claimed the ones we love, we have to ultimately
accept circumstances and move toward forgiveness. If we don't, we will
stay in what author David A. Seamands refers to in *Healing for Damaged
Emotions* as "frozen rage."[1] Of course we are going to feel anger at the
injustice and unfairness of certain events in our lives, but holding on to
pain is like drinking poison. The only antidote for resentment is forgiveness.

In *The Gift of Forgiveness*, Charles Stanley writes, "Holding on to hurt
is like grabbing a rattlesnake by the tail; you are going to be bitten. As
the poison of bitterness works its way through many facets of your per-
sonality, death will occur—death that is far more reaching than your
physical death, for it has the potential to destroy those around you as
well."[2]

Forgiveness is the key that Christ offers us all. He came to set us free
so that our hearts can fully embrace the present and the future. The
Bible tells us in Galatians 5:22, "But the Spirit produces the fruit of love,
joy, peace, patience, kindness, goodness, faithfulness" (NCV). A friend
once told me that the way to measure your recovery process is to exam-
ine the fruits of the Spirit in your life. Are you experiencing these on a
daily basis? What is your life producing? If you are grounded in frozen
rage and depression over losses, if your life is filled with bitterness and
vengeful thoughts, then you are not living in freedom. Forgiveness can
enable you to produce these fruits of the Spirit.

In my own experience, when I was able to forgive, I began to experience these fruits of the Spirit once again. I had been stuck in depression
for months because of the bitterness I was harboring in my heart. When
we don't forgive, when we don't accept the losses in our lives, we are not
living; we are merely existing.

FORGIVING GOD

Many people who have experienced great loss remain bitter and resentful toward God, believing He is responsible for all of their problems when things don't work out the way they had planned. We often wonder how a good and loving God could permit such pain. Why would the Creator allow such anarchy in our lives? If God loved us as much as He says He does, then He would stop the pain and make everything right again, wouldn't He? When God doesn't cater to our demands, we inevitably become angry with Him.

In *A Grief Observed*, C. S. Lewis writes, "The terrible thing is that a perfectly good God is in this matter hardly less formidable than a Cosmic Sadist. The more we believe that God hurts only to heal, the less we can believe that there is any use in bidding for tenderness. A cruel man might be bribed—might grow tired of his vile sport—might have a temporary fit of mercy, as alcoholics have fits of sobriety. But suppose that what you are up against is a surgeon whose intentions are wholly good. The kinder and more conscientious he is, the inexorable he will go on cutting. If he yielded to your entreaties, if he stopped before the operation was complete, all the pain up to that point would have been useless."[3]

You see, all of us are on an operating table before God. Some of us have been begging Him to stop the pain, yet He continues to cut away. And so we begin to harbor resentment against Him, believing He is hurting, not healing us. We don't understand that as we lay bleeding before Him, He continues to cut because, as C. S. Lewis puts it, "He is wholly good." God is kind and conscientious of our lives and our futures. If He were to interrupt His work now, if He were to yield to our cries to stop the pain, then every hurt we've felt up to this point would be useless. We will face brutal times in our lives. But our God is wholly good, and He is orchestrating every step so we may live a full life and one day look back and see just how good He is.

One of the staff members at Restore Ministries lost her brother to cancer six years ago. He was eighteen years old when he died. She told me she couldn't understand why God would let something like this happen to a child, to someone who had so much life ahead of him. Her stepfather struggled desperately with the grief of losing his only son, wondering what he'd done to bring such a terrible punishment to his family. This tragedy turned the family upside down with anger and grief. But shortly after the death of her brother, her stepfather gave his life to Christ because of the apparent relationship his son had with God.

When we go through a trial, our job is to draw out what joy can be found, allowing perseverance to finish the work of maturity. But the first thing that usually comes to mind when we are facing trials is, *Why me?* Asking why brings up the age-old question of God's all-powerfulness versus Satan's power to make us suffer. There are countless volumes devoted to this deep theological subject, and I encourage you to read and explore it further. But in this study our focus is not to explain the problem of pain, but to show how God brings good out of it.

C. S. Lewis wrote, "In the fallen and partially redeemed universe we may distinguish (1) the simple good descending from God, (2) the simple evil produced by rebellious creatures, and (3) the exploitation of that evil by God for His redemptive purpose, which produces (4) the complex good to which accepted suffering and repented sin contribute."[4] The way God exploits the problem of pain in the world for His redemptive purpose is our focal point. When we look for redemption, we focus on what good is coming out of a trial more than the disaster of it. God's joy is the center of our activity and purpose.

I attended the funeral of a young man that had committed suicide. When the pastor got up to speak, his message profoundly impacted me. He said that the problem with young people committing suicide is that they haven't lived long enough to experience how things change over time—that losses in our lives eventually give way to new beginnings. This is a significant step in helping us move forward in the grief process.

Betty Jo's Story

"I would never say that I was glad that Daniel died, but out of his death came a relationship with God that I'd never had before and could never have had without a loss like that. It's sad that it took this for me to see God in all of His glory. My dad died when I was twenty-eight—it was sudden. He had lung cancer with barely any symptoms and died four months later. Before my father's death, I saw God as this being up in heaven who watched for all my wrongs, so that He could judge me—like a teacher who would whack you over the head when you did something wrong. I served Him out of fear—not respect, but fear. But when my dad died, I searched and I read, and I got into the Bible for the first time. This is when God became my father. As He says, He is "a father to the fatherless."[5]

"Even though I was young woman, God became my father. I saw Him in a much more loving role, and a present role—because my dad had been a very big influence in my life. He was always there for me, and I always respected my dad and loved him.

"Then my mother died twenty years later. She had been one of my best friends. God became even bigger to me after my mother died. Still, in both of those losses I had my husband, who was my best friend. It seemed like he could read when I was missing them and when I needed encouragement. I remember once we were driving down the road and he just patted my hand, because it was a sad day. I didn't even know he knew, but he did. He said, 'I miss her too.' But when Dan died, I didn't have anyone that close, and that's when I really had to trust God's hand—the unseen hand—and believe that it was really there. I had to believe that it would hold mine when I was lonely, that He would be there in the darkest nights when I didn't know what to do. That's when you have to trust what you've read. And when you trust, He comes through for you."

FORGIVING OURSELVES

The last part of the forgiveness process is perhaps the most powerful and often the most needed: forgiving ourselves for the mistakes we've made, the pain we have caused to ourselves and to others around us. I had to deal with this type of forgiveness firsthand during my recovery process. For many years I was angry with myself. My childhood dreams had failed because of my many addictions and personal struggles. *I* was the reason for my failure, the reason my life had crumbled around me. There seemed to be no way I could forgive myself for these horrible acts in my past.

Yet, like the pastor who spoke about the kid that committed suicide, I have now lived long enough and have experienced how God has worked all those painful things in my life for good. I would have never written this book had God yielded to all my bargaining and pleading with Him because of the horrible decisions I made. I hated myself for the things I did, the shame I lived in, and the loss it created in my life. The loss of respect and integrity was unbearable for me to face. The depression I was trapped in for so long was like a thick cloud around me; I could not see past it.

At the core of my addictions and problems was a deep resentment toward myself. It was difficult to believe that I would ever come out of it. I could not escape the feeling that nothing good could ever come out of my life. I believe I had irreparably ruined it. But as time went on and I began to look at my life through the rearview mirror, I could see how God truly had worked all things for good. Even the things that I never thought I could ever forgive myself for, the things that I was so ashamed of in my past, God has now allowed me to use in helping other people who are going through difficulties. You see, God never wastes a hurt.

One day in a twelve-step meeting, I encountered the term *powerlessness.* We were studying how we are powerless over our human condition and how our lives had become unmanageable. As the weeks went on, powerlessness eventually led us to all the things in our lives that we had done wrong, to the fact that we were powerless over all of it. All the sin, shame, guilt, consequences—there is nothing we can do about it. So what blessing comes from not having any power over all this? The ability to give up control. Eventually I began to get it. It was as if God was saying, "Scott you are powerless over all this; be still and know that I am your God."

That admission was the key that unlocked the hope for a new beginning in my life—a faint inner belief that there could be a purpose, a goodness, from this wreckage that I had been in. I had finally taken ownership and understood that I could be blessed. At that moment, I recognized my need for God. And from that experience, over twelve years ago, has come this incredible new life. Now I have witnessed personally how God can use everything that has happened to me for the good of His kingdom. All the bad, all the pain, all the hurt—He used it.

REFLECTION QUESTIONS

Who or what in your life have you not forgiven and why? How has this unforgiveness affected your life?

How does forgiveness set us free and heal our hearts?

Looking back, was there ever a time in your life that you were blaming God? Describe the situation.

Do you believe that God works all things for good? Explain how you have experienced this in your life.

List some of the blessings God has showered on you.

Why is it sometimes harder for us to forgive ourselves than others? Is there something you are struggling to forgive yourself for?

REFLECTIONS

REFLECTIONS

REFLECTIONS

CHAPTER SIX

ACCEPTANCE: A NEW DAY

The final stage of the grieving process is making peace with what has happened. Once we have forgiven with God's help, we have a sense of completeness in our grief. This is acceptance. It is here, in this stage of acceptance, that we are finally able to acknowledge our loss and grieve all that was lost with it. When all has been resolved, we are open to hope, healing, and a new beginning for our lives.

Acceptance is essential in the grieving process. If we never move into this stage, if we stay behind in our grief, it will keep us from living life to the fullest. Living in grief keeps us from the people and things that are in the present. If we're trapped in the past, we'll miss out on everyone and everything that is still moving forward.

In the previous chapter we introduced the concept of powerlessness, and how it can be the beginning of hope. If loss is inevitable in life, then we must also come to terms with the inevitability of the loss of control over our lives. The reality of our human existence is that we don't have control over much. It is an illusion to believe we can control our lives entirely. In reality, we only have control over our response to the circumstances of life.

If we can finally lay down our own agenda, our own control tactics, we can find hope in the idea that we don't have to try so hard to keep things perfect. God is good, and even when we can't see it, He's constantly working to bring good from our trials. When we come to terms with our powerlessness, we are able to experience new hope.

In the twelve steps of Alcoholics Anonymous, the step following powerlessness deals with the question of faith. It says we come to believe "that a power greater than ourselves can restore us to sanity."[1] In essence, this step is about defining what we believe about God. Do we believe in His goodness, and, ultimately, do we truly believe He is in control of our lives? Do we believe that He can be trusted?

The third step, which comes after we have wrestled with our belief about God, reads, "We made the decision to turn our will and our lives over to the care of God."[2] We cannot turn our will and our lives over to the care of God unless we first trust Him. If we don't believe He can and will make good from our lives, then it will be nearly impossible for us to turn our lives over to Him.

So let's look once again at all three of these steps and how they relate to our grieving process. First, God asks me to recognize the great limitations I have as a human being. I always think of the admission of powerlessness as the ultimate position of humility. Admission is a confession. The step calls for us to *admit* that we need God to do for us what we cannot do for ourselves. In humility, we acknowledge that we do not have the power to control our own lives. It is not a coincidence that people come to Restore Ministries after a painful loss. Loss brings to light the lack of control we have over our lives. The irony is that the more we try to regain control, the more we lose it.

In the second step, we struggle with what we believe about God. Do we believe that He can be trusted to be in control of our lives? This step causes us to contemplate whether we believe in the greater goodness of God. In the third step, we have come to a place in our hearts where we know God is good and can be trusted with our lives and our losses. This is the action step—where we actually give God all our hurts and losses. We have to see past the tragedies, past the great losses and shattered dreams, as well as the despair and bitter losses. We must understand that God will bring good from our loss. Philippians 1:6 says, "God began doing a good work in you, and I am sure he will continue it until it is finished when Jesus Christ comes again" (NCV). In all things God promises completion. His works will never go unfinished. Our losses, tragedies, and shattered dreams all have a time to be completed under heaven. They will all be used to bring about good because He promises it. We can trust Him with our lives and our losses, knowing He will finish what has been started.

Betty Jo's Story

"I've seen God use this whole experience in my life to help me reach out to others. I was at the cemetery one day, visiting Daniel's grave, and I noticed a woman there. She had lost her own husband, and she was having a hard time. I'm normally someone who needs to be asked before I start talking, but she looked like she was in those first few days after a death, so I felt moved to talk with her. And after talking with her, she told me, 'You know, I know God brought me here today, because I never come on this day, I never come at this time—I know God wanted you to talk to me today.'

"There's a verse that says He's the God of all comfort who comforts us in our tribulations, so that we may comfort others with the comfort he has given us.[3] I'd always clung to the part that says He's the God who comforts us, but after talking to that lady, the last part of the Scripture—'so that we can comfort others.'—took on new meaning. I knew God wanted me to comfort other women who'd lost their husbands. I felt God was leading me down a different path, and I started looking at it not as a loss, but as something that I was actually gaining. It was an excitement over what God was going to do and how I could help Him heal hearts that had suffered a loss like mine."

The ultimate acceptance in the grieving process involves understanding that our lives are not our own. As believers, we have given our lives to God so that we may bring glory to Him. Acceptance is embracing God's purposes through and for our lives. When we face profound losses, we have to dig deep to see that God is a redeeming God. He can and will bring good and glory through our trials. When we allow Him access to our broken lives, we will find Him under the rubble, working and cleaning so that we may see His light through the darkness.

When we embrace all that God can do through our loss, it brings joy. It is not merely about finding meaning in the pain; it is about finding *God* in the pain. Acceptance is not resignation; it is embracing the good that God is able to bring from our broken lives.

REFLECTION QUESTIONS

How has a lack of faith in God caused you distress?

How might admitting powerlessness over your life ultimately lead to hope?

Can you trust God to control all aspects of your life? Explain.

What do you believe is the difference between happiness and joy?

Where are you in the grief process today?

REFLECTIONS

REFLECTIONS

REFLECTIONS

REFLECTIONS

MY PERSONAL PLAN OF CHANGE

SAMPLE PLAN OF CHANGE

You are going to create a daily plan to allow God to give you relief from your grief and loss. Whether your loss is new or you have been dealing with this grief for far too long, this plan will help you begin some steps to get on the road to healing and acceptance. You will begin the process by briefly describing your loss and what stage of grief you think you are in at the present time. You will have to be completely open and vulnerable about what you are and have been going through. Think about whether you are suppressing the voice of your loss and declare right now that you will be willing to make the changes necessary to get through this process. Then you will list and contact a dependable set of people to support you in what you are about to do. They should be safe, they should be supportive and visionary, they should be encouraging, and they should be willing to keep you accountable to keep moving on the days that you feel less than hopeful. They should be made thoroughly acquainted with you and your loss. You will want to write down your goals for how you can begin today to move through the stages of grief so that you will be able to come out on the other side and move into acceptance. You will want to write down your fears and emotions about what is to come by allowing yourself to be honest about your pain. You will also write out what your vision for your life will be like when you have completed the grieving process. Remember that there is no timetable for going through the grieving process. Allow yourself room to grieve when need be and rejoice when there is times of triumph through the trials.

Read through the following sample Personal Plan of Change before completing your own plan.

Self-Assessment: My name is Beth and I am thirty-three years old. I am on the verge of being divorced. I never expected my life to turn out this way. I had been happily married for ten years and never thought that divorce was possible in our marriage. But the bottom fell out and our marriage and has tragically ended in divorce. First I was in denial, but now I feel like I am stuck in anger, bitterness and resentment toward myself, my husband, God, and the world.

I am so angry that I am even in this situation. I did everything that I could to keep my life intact with my husband and children. And now he has decided to leave me. I just don't understand why. I loved my husband so much and never would want to be without him. I miss him every day and don't think that I can get past this pain. But mostly I am just angry.

I struggle with what life is going to be like now. I hate getting up in the morning. I hate facing the day. My children are suffering and that is hard to deal with because I don't even know how to deal with my own grief. But I am required to be strong and I don't know how to do that when I feel like my life has come to a screeching halt. What are all my holidays going to be like from now on, will I be constantly reminded of the life that I no longer have? I just don't know how I will ever accept the fact that I have lost my marriage and my future with the man that I loved more than life. The life that I knew, loved, and counted on is over. This loss seems unbearable. Why? Why did this have to happen to me?

Step One: List Your Issues

Spirit (for example, anger toward God, blame, despair, disconnection):

I am angry with God about this whole situation. I don't understand why he would let my marriage fail. I feel like a part of me has died and I don't know if I will ever be able to return to normal. I don't know even what I believe in anymore.

Mind (for example, self-loathing, bitterness toward others, obsessions):
This divorce, this devastation, is consuming my every thought. I can't think about anything else. All the memories and good times are surfacing and leaving me in a chronic stage of despair. My mind is a battlefield.

Body (for example, unhealthy lifestyle, cycle of habit, depression):
Since everything has happened, life has turned unmanageable. Getting out of bed, exercising, or anything that forces me to use any more energy seems useless. I feel like my body has paid part of the price also through this. Just like my marriage, my body feels as if it's falling apart too.

Step Two: Goals

Spirit: I am going to make an effort to allow God to work through this loss in my life. I will admit that I am powerless to change my circumstances and that God has complete control over my life. I will do my best to believe that He is good and that He does work all things out for the good of those who love Him. I will begin to be dependent on Him instead of my own ways of trying to fix my pain.

Mind: I don't want to constantly remind myself of my loneliness. I want to be able to think about the positive things I have in my life and what I have to look forward to with my children. In the morning and in the evening I will meditate on the verses from the Bible about how my life can bring joy and peace in the midst of suffering.

Body: I will begin to walk and get physical exercise to help me release some of my anxiety about the future. Walking will also help release endorphins that will create a sense of well-being and help combat the depression that I am struggling with. I will seek some of my close friends to walk with me and that will be positive time of support and encouragement.

Step Three: Support Groups and Individuals

Support community:
>   Women's Small Group at church
>   DivorceCare program

Individual Support:
>   Suzie (mentor)
>   Gretchen (long-time close friend and supporter)
>   my sister Laurie
>   my pastor
>   mom and dad

Step Four: Your Vision

When I finally come out on the other side from this pain and loss that I am going through, I will be able to move forward into the future with my children and my heart will be open to new beginnings. I will be able to rely on God and believe that He has a plan for the rest of my life. I will want to start a small group for women that are divorced or are going through a divorce. I will want to share my story with others in the hope that someone else might find peace in knowing that their struggle with this loss can produce joy, hope, and healing. I want my children to know that they have a mommy that loves them, and I want to be a role model for them, a source of inspiration and hope. This can only happen if I am fully present in a life that has a future. I will have peace and joy as I accept the past and the loss. With god holding my hand I will move into the future. I will have a life that produces great fruit.

Step Five: Your Prayer

Lord, I know that I have put my trust in myself for so long to fix the pain that I have been feeling from this divorce. I know now that I can't do this life without You to pull me through. I am not strong enough to pull myself out of this pit of depression and sadness. I cannot see a positive future for myself without Your help. I cannot love my family the way I should without Your deliverance from this grief. Father I pray that You give me the strength and courage to walk one day at a time with You, allowing You to heal my heart, heal my past, and lead me into a new day with you guiding me every step of the way. Amen.

CREATING YOUR PERSONAL PLAN OF CHANGE

Your Story:

Write out a paragraph or two describing your journey so far through the grieving process. Talk openly about the loss that you have experienced in your life. *(What has been the hardest part to cope with? What are some of your deepest fears about your loss or your future? What has prevented you from moving forward in your grief up to this point? What stage of the grieving process do you think you are currently in?)*

Step One: List Your Issues

Spirit (for example, anger toward God, blame, despair, disconnection)

Mind (for example, self-loathing, bitterness toward others, obsessions)

Body (for example, diets, unhealthy lifestyle, cycle of habit, depression)

Step Two: Goals

Write out individual goals for each issue that you have struggled with, and specific steps that you will take with God's help.

Spirit

Mind

Body

Step 3: Support Groups and Individuals

Find a support community. Below are resources that can help you in this quest.

Restore Ministries (www.restoreymca.org)
Caring Resources (www.caringresources.com)
Grief Share (www.griefshare.org)
DivorceCare (www.divorcecare.com)
Alcoholics Anonymous (www.alcoholics-anonymous.org)
Overeaters Anonymous (www.oa.org)
Sexaholics Anonymous (www.saa-recovery.org)
Al Anon (www.al-anon.org)
Narcotics Anonymous (www.na.org)
Other:

Find individuals to support you. List at least one individual in each category below who will support you and share your journey to recovery.

Friend:
Sponsor:
Therapist:
Counselor:
Doctor:
Pastor:
Life Coach:
Personal Trainer:
Nutritionist:
Physical Therapist:
Other:

Step Four: Your Vision

Write a description of what your life will be like when you are finally through the grieving process, and how you can live your life to the fullest.

Step Five: Your Prayer

Only God can give you the freedom you seek. Write a prayer that you can say every day while you are working through this liberation from the grief and loss that seems all consuming at times.

During the courses of our lives, we will all experience loss. Some losses will be minor, such as not hitting a ball when the bases are loaded; others will be life changing, such as a divorce or the death of a loved one. To live is to experience loss. There is nothing that we can hold onto forever; everything ultimately comes to an end. My hope is that this book has helped you understand the powerful healing process God has designed for us. Continue to push through and surround yourself with fellow travelers who can support you.

God bless you as He leads you on your journey to hope, health, and happiness.

TIPS FOR LEADING A JOURNEY TO FREEDOM SMALL GROUP

Welcome and thank you for accepting the challenge of leading others along their own journeys to freedom. These tips are designed to aid you in creating a small group setting that is productive and full of hope, health, and happiness.

PREPARATION

Being well prepared will help alleviate any anxiety you may have about leading your group. When you know what you want to accomplish in your group, it will help you stay on track with the lesson plan. Plus, if you're not prepared, participants will pick up on your lack of preparation, which might affect their own dedication to the group and the process of change. In extreme cases, lack of preparation may even cause you to lose some participants. If the leader is not committed, why should the participants be committed? So come to your group prepared to lead them.

Be a role model. A good facilitator is simply a model group participant. Be on time. Be prepared. Do your homework. Guard against moodiness.

Be consistent. Be positive. Be a good listener. Maintain confidentiality. Be enthusiastic.

Recognize your limitations. It is important that you remember that you are not responsible for the results of your group. You are not responsible to "fix" anyone. You are not a counselor, a therapist, or a minister. You are a mentor, one who is helping guide another down a path that you have traveled before. Each participant is responsible for his or her own life and journey.

OPENING THE GROUP SESSION

Use gentleness and patience as you pace the progress of the group. Rushing through the lessons might be exhausting for your participants. Try to find some kind of meaningful devotional, excerpt from a book, or song to emphasize and complement what you are studying for the week.

Plan your time so that you are able to get through the majority of the recommended questions in each less on, but more important, be prepared to settle for quality of questions and answers over quantity. The goal is to have a productive meeting. Getting through every question in the lesson may seem optimal, but it may not accomplish the goal.

BE AWARE

Avoid being the center of attention during group time. Your role as leader is to get the group involved in sharing, to keep the discussion moving forward and on topic, and to make sure that your group is on time and the necessary material is covered. You are there to give direction and guidance to the group, but avoid dominating the group by talking too much in the sessions.

Be aware of your group dynamics. As a facilitator, get to know your group members. In order to help them as much as possible, you need to be aware and in tune with their needs. Pay attention to the members' body language, their actions, and what they are saying and sharing. Assess the participants in their response and in their openness (or lack of).

Don't let any one member dominate the group. Handling the "talker" in your group will require some skill. Be careful, because if one member begins to dominate your group, it can alienate some of the more reserved members. If one member is opening up and sharing for long periods of time, try not to let this member's problems control the group. Say, "I would love to continue this discussion with you after the meeting. Will that be okay?" This will keep you from appearing uncaring and will give the group permission to get back on track. Also, think about positioning. Sit beside these individuals instead of across from them to avoid prolonged eye contact. When presenting a question or topic for discussion, put a time limit on responses. If someone runs over the limit, don't be afraid to break in and praise the person's point, but then raise a new question back to the group about what was shared. Validate the individual's feelings and input, but then focus the discussion.

Allow silence. Often, facilitators become uncomfortable with silence in group discussions. Sometimes it is good to have a moment of silence so that the participants will speak up and start owning the conversation. Do not feel like you have to fill the void. If the group members think you are going to fill the silence, then they will learn to wait for you. If you find that there has been a considerable amount of time given to answer a question and no one is speaking up, you might ask them why they are silent or move on to another question.

Contain the desire to rescue. If someone gets emotionally upset or begins to cry and show emotion during the session, avoid anything that could interfere with the member feeling the emotion of the moment. Let the individual express the emotions and deal with them, even if they are painful. While the person is sharing, do not reach over and hug, touch, or comfort. After the individual has finished sharing and is done, then offer a hug if you desire or thank and affirm the person for speaking courageously.

Use self-disclosure appropriately. One element of being a good facilitator is a willingness to be vulnerable and to share your journey of change at the appropriate times. However, be careful that you do not use the group to deal with your unresolved issues.

As you lead discussion, consistently state and reiterate the boundaries of group discussion—confidentiality about what is spoken in the group, respect for each other, and the right to pass if a member doesn't feel comfortable sharing at the time. Accept what each person has to say without making sudden judgments. Be the primary catalyst in providing a warm, open, trusting, and caring atmosphere. This will help the group gradually take ownership.

CLOSING THE GROUP

Manage your time wisely. It is important that your group start and end on time. Strive for consistency, beginning with the first meeting by starting and ending on time and continuing that schedule each week.

SESSION ONE—INTRODUCTION WEEK

Lesson Goal:

In your first meeting you will not cover any material. You will begin to get to know each other as a group and learn the structure and guidelines for the next eight weeks, as well as the expectations of each participant.

Leading the Session:

Welcome the participants and commend them on taking this action to pursue change in their lives.

Ask each participant to share whatever information they are

comfortable sharing about themselves with the group: name, occupation, number and ages of children and or grandchildren, where you were born, how you heard of this group, etc. are good places to start. Be sure that you and your co-facilitator (if applicable) introduce yourselves first to increase the group's comfort level.

Show the first session of Scott Reall's video (if applicable), talk about what they have to look forward to as a group in the upcoming eight weeks, and present group guidelines to the participants:

Confidentiality is of the utmost importance.
Group members are not required to talk but encouraged to do so.
Agree to accept each other and to encourage one another.
We do not give advice, or try to "fix" or rescue other group members.
Be honest.
Be on time.
Agree to make the weekly meetings and the daily work a priority.

Ask if anyone would like to ask a question or add a group guideline. The goal is for participants to feel safe, secure and encouraged.

Choose one of the following warm-up questions to open up the group and begin to break the ice:

What do you like to do when you have free time?
What brings you great joy?
What is a special talent or skill that you possess?

Pair your group into couples, and give each person five minutes to answer the following questions to each other:

What brought you here today?
What in your life do you want to change?
What excuses will you give yourself to not come to group or do your homework?

Closing the Group

Encourage the group members to come back to the next meeting.

Encourage group members to read and answer the questions at the end of the chapter to be discussed next week and to write their answers in the blank space provided. Tell them to come next week ready to discuss.

Assign accountability partners for each participant and, if possible, pair them with the partner that they were paired with for the last exercise. Ask them to exchange phone numbers and e-mail addresses.

Accountability Partner Guidelines:

Discuss the specifics of the change each person is trying to achieve.

Relate how each person is doing in spirit, mind, and body.

Ask your partner about his or her struggles, problems, and particular difficulties.

Be considerate of each other's time and situations, and remember that the purpose is to discuss change.

Make an effort to take the conversation beyond a superficial level.

The Importance of Accountability Partners:

One of the best tools to help us through the rough times in our journey to freedom is accountability. Often we don't realize how much accountability has influenced and affected our decisions throughout our lives. We are accountable to get to work on time or we may lose our jobs. In school, athletes have to keep their grades up, attend class, and get to practice or they are off the team. In the same way, unless we have some sort of accountability, many of us will not sustain our efforts to change. We need accountability to develop the discipline of sticking with something, especially if consistency is hard for us.

Be sure and thank them for coming this week. Express how excited you are to be with them and to discover where this journey is going to take all of you as a group.

Close with prayer, singing, saying the serenity prayer, or any positive way you feel appropriate.

SESSIONS 2 THROUGH 7—COVERING THE STUDY GUIDE MATERIAL

For these six weeks, you will be covering Chapters 1 through 6 in the study guide. You will want to follow and review the guidelines for preparing for leading a small group. Once each session begins thank everyone for being there and then begin to go over that week's readings and have members share about what stood out to them in the lesson. You will then want to go over the questions at the end of the chapter for the rest of your time. If some do not want to share their answers, do not force them. Thank everyone that shares for participating and encourage those that don't. Encourage members to use the Reflection pages at he end of each chapter during the week for journaling and notes. End in prayer.

SESSION 8—CREATING PERSONAL PLANS OF CHANGE

Leading the Session:

Go over the group guidelines for respecting participants as they share their plans.

Have participants read action plans aloud.

Have them sign the places provided in their books, committing them to follow the plans of action they have created.

Talk about the specific next steps that they can take (for example, enrolling in a twelve-steps or other recovery program or a personal training or exercise program).

Make sure they have all the resources they need to fulfill their action plans.

Thank them for coming and close in prayer.

Hold hands and sing "Amazing Grace."

Introduction

1. "Memorable Quotes for On the Waterfront," Internet Movie Database, http://www.imdb.com/title/tt0047296/quotes.
2. Archibald D. Hart, *Unmasking Male Depression* (Nashville, TN: Thomas Nelson, 2001), 125.
3. *The Mentor Book of Major American Poets*, ed. Oscar Williams and Edward Taylor (New York: New American Library, 1962), 69.
4. Sheryl Cooke and Farah Moore, *From Hurt to Hope* (Nashville, TN: Caring Resources, 1982), 8.

Chapter One

1. John W. James and Russell Friedman, *The Grief Recovery Handbook: The Action Program for Moving Beyond Death, Divorce, and Other Losses* (New York: HarperCollins, 1998).
2. Proverbs 29:18 KJV.
3. Larry Crabb, *Shattered Dreams: God's Unexpected Pathway to Joy* (Colorado Springs, CO:Waterbrook, 2002).
4. Cooke and Moore, *From Hurt to Hope*, 8.
5. "Richard Burton Lyrics—Camelot (Reprise)," STLyrics.com, http://www.stlyrics.com/lyrics/camelot/camelotreprise.htm.
6. Harry Emerson Fosdick, *Riverside Sermons* (New York: Harper & Brothers, 1958), 54.
7. Henri Nouwen, *Turn My Mourning Into Dancing* (Nashville: W Publishing, 2001), 35.

Chapter Two

1. Chip Dodd, *The Voice of the Heart: A Call to Full Living* (Franklin, TN: Sage Hill Resources, 2001), 43.

Chapter Three

1. Robert Hemfelt, Frank Minirth, Paul Meier, Brian Newman, and Deborah Newman, *Love Is a Choice Workbook* (Nashville, TN: Thomas Nelson, 2004), 189.

Chapter 4

1. Robert Hemfelt, Frank Minirth, Paul Meier, Brian Newman, and Deborah Newman, *Love Is a Choice Workbook* (Nashville, TN: Thomas Nelson, 2004), 191.
2. "Memorable Quotes for City of Angels," Internet Movie Database, http://imdb.com/title/tt0120632/quotes.
3. Chip Dodd, *The Voice of the Heart: A Call to Full Living* (Franklin, TN: Sage Hill Resources, 2001), 59.
4. Ibid.
5. Ibid, 68.

6. George Sheehan, M.D., *Personal Best: The Foremost Philosopher of Fitness Shares Techniques and Tactics for Success and Self-Liberation* (New York: Rodale Press, 1992), 218.

7. Sue Monk Kidd, *When the Heart Waits: Spiritual Direction for Life's Sacred Questions* (New York: HarperOne, 2006), 4.

8. Sheehan, 233.

Chapter Five

1. David A. Seamands, *Healing for Damaged Emotions: Recovering from the Memories That Cause Our Pain* (Colorado Springs, CO: Chariot Victory Publishing, 1981).

2. Charles Stanley, *The Gift of Forgiveness* (Nashville, TN: Thomas Nelson, 1991), 11.

3. C. S. Lewis, *A Grief Observed* (New York: HarperOne, 2001), 49–50.

4. C. S. Lewis, *The Problem of Pain* (New York: Simon & Schuster, 1996; reprint New York: Macmillian, 1962), 98–99.

5. Psalm 68:5 NIV.

Chapter Six

1. Alcoholics Anonymous World Services, Inc., *Twelve Steps and Twelve Traditions* (Center City, MN: Hazelden, 2002), 25.

2. Ibid, 34.

3. 2 Corinthians 1:3–4 NCV.